SHIFNAL

A Pictorial History

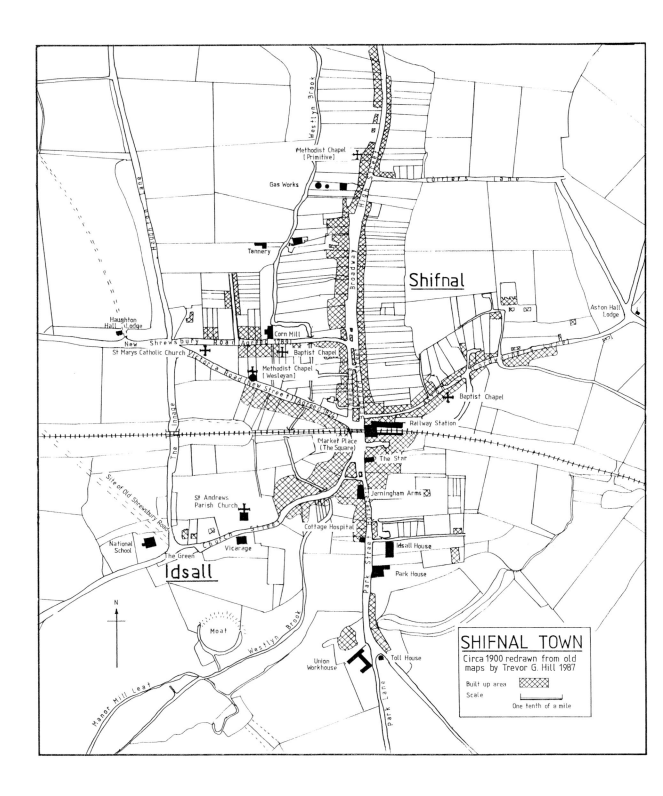

Westlyn Brook

Corriers Lane

Methodist Chapel
[Primitive]

Gas Works

Tannery

Shifnal

Haughton
Hall Lodge

Aston Hall
Lodge

New Shrewsbury Road Agreed
Corn Mill

St Marys Catholic Church

Baptist Chapel

Victoria Road New Street Agreed

Methodist Chapel
[Wesleyan]

Baptist Chapel

The Innage

Railway Station

Market Place
(The Square)

Site of Old Shrewsbury Road

The Star

St Andrews
Parish Church

Jerningham Arms

National
School

Cottage Hospital

Idsall House

The Green

Church Street

Vicarage

Park Street

Park House

Idsall

N

Westlyn Brook

Moat

Union
Workhouse

Toll House

Manor Mill Leat

Park Lane

SHIFNAL TOWN

Circa 1900 redrawn from old
maps by Trevor G. Hill 1987

Built up area

Scale

One tenth of a mile

SHIFNAL
A Pictorial History

Edited by

Sylvia Watts

Phillimore

1989

Published by
PHILLIMORE & CO. LTD.
Shopwyke Hall, Chichester, Sussex

ISBN 0 85033 686 4

Printed and bound in Great Britain by
BIDDLES LTD.
Guildford, Surrey

To the people of Shifnal, past and present

List of Illustrations

Illustration Acknowledgements

St Andrew's Archive Group is most grateful to the following people for their generosity in allowing us to use their photographs. We have not attributed particular photographs to individuals because, in many cases, we have been given several copies of the same photograph by different people and it would seem invidious to name one person rather than another: Mrs. P. Bothwell, Mrs. M. Boulton, Mrs. A. Clarke, Miss K. Cox, Mr. R. Davies, the late R. Dawson, Mr. A. Dean, Mrs. J. Dean, Mrs. M. Doyle, Mrs. L. Evans, Miss E. Gardiner, Mr. Glews, Mrs. M. Harris-Edge, Mr. and Mrs. F. Jeffrey, Mrs. K. Jeffreys, Mr. R. Law, Mr. and Mrs. G. Lowe, Mrs. T. McNeill, Mrs. C. Marshall, Mr. G. Nickless, Miss E. Phillips, Miss O. Phillips, Mrs. Picken, Mr. W. Preece, Mrs. L. Spencer, Miss S. Swinburne, Mr. R. Turnock, Mrs. M. Weaver, Mrs. J. and the late Mr. J. Williams, and Mr. J. Williamson. We are also grateful to the Local Studies Library, Shrewsbury, for permission to use photographs 13, 22, 24, 26, 42, and 43, and prints 2, 18, 69, 71 and 146; to Stafford Joint Record Office for the poster 116, and to *The Times* for photographs 129 and 130.

Acknowledgements

Mrs. Sylvia Watts would like to thank the following people for their help in researching the captions for the pictures. Firstly and especially Miss O. Phillips, whose remarkable memory of Shifnal people has been invaluable; also the staff of the Local Studies Library, Shrewsbury, and Mrs. P. Bothwell, Mrs. J. Guest, Mrs. M. Hill, Mr. T. Hill, Mr. F. Jones, Mrs. C. Marshall, Mrs. M. Robinson, Mrs. L. Spencer and Mr. R. Turnock.

Introduction

Shifnal is a small town/large village, with a population of about six thousand lying in East Shropshire in undulating and productive countryside. Though now to a large extent a dormitory town for people working in Wolverhampton and Telford with only a small market and shopping centre, for most of its life as a community it has fulfilled the function of a market for the surrounding agricultural area.

Shifnal town – the subject of most of the photographs in this book – is the centre of a large agricultural parish which was formerly scattered with small farming hamlets dependent upon the church, market and craftsmen of Shifnal town. Most of the hamlets are now reduced to single farmsteads, or the area of the hamlet fields has become the park or estate of a large house, as at Aston and Hatton. In the early 18th century about half the population of the parish lived in the town and the other half in the various hamlets. Today the population of the parish is much more concentrated into the town. These large multi-township parishes are typical of the area.

Shifnal town and most of the hamlets must have originated as settlements in Saxon times judging by place-name evidence but, as with many towns and villages, the first substantial documentary record is in Domesday Book. In 1086 Shifnal was apparently a relatively prosperous and well-populated community. It had suffered greatly as a result of the suppression of the revolt of the Earls of Mercia and Northumberland against William the Conqueror, but it fairly quickly recovered. Along with most of Shropshire, Shifnal was given by the Conqueror to Roger de Montgomery, Earl of Shrewsbury.

Shifnal continued to prosper through the Middle Ages, and more land was brought into cultivation to support the growing population. The settlements of Woodhouses and Priorslee developed as clearings in the forests which spread across most of the western part of the parish. In 1245 Walter de Dunstanville III, then lord of the manor, obtained a charter from the king allowing a weekly market and yearly fair. The main elements of the present street plan of the centre of Shifnal were almost certainly established at about this time, when the north-south axis of a wide market street with long building plots (burgage plots) fronting onto it was added to the older Church Street area near the river crossing and church. This market presumably prospered, as a further charter was obtained in 1315. The 1327 Lay Subsidy returns show a flourishing community. The size and beauty of the church, which was mainly built in its present form in the 13th and 14th centuries, certainly suggest a prosperous community, or the favour of the lord of the manor, or both.

In fact, Shifnal has never had a resident lord of the manor; it has always been just one manor amongst the many belonging to a wealthy landowner. Absentee landlords have not, however, led to freedom and independence; Shifnal's lords have always had efficient administrators who exercised close seigneurial supervision. In spite of possessing such urban characteristics as market charters and burgage tenure, Shifnal never became a fully self-governing town. Remnants of feudalism lingered very late in Shifnal. The yearly fair was a manorial prerogative with the lord of the manor taking the tolls until the 19th century. Mulcture and suit of mill, whereby tenants had to have their corn ground at the lord of the manor's mill and pay for this with a proportion of the grain, was a feature of leases well into the 18th century. The medieval tax of heriot which entitled the lord of the manor to a tenant's best beast after his death was still levied in the 18th century, though it was commuted to a money payment. Manorial legal functions such as court leets and

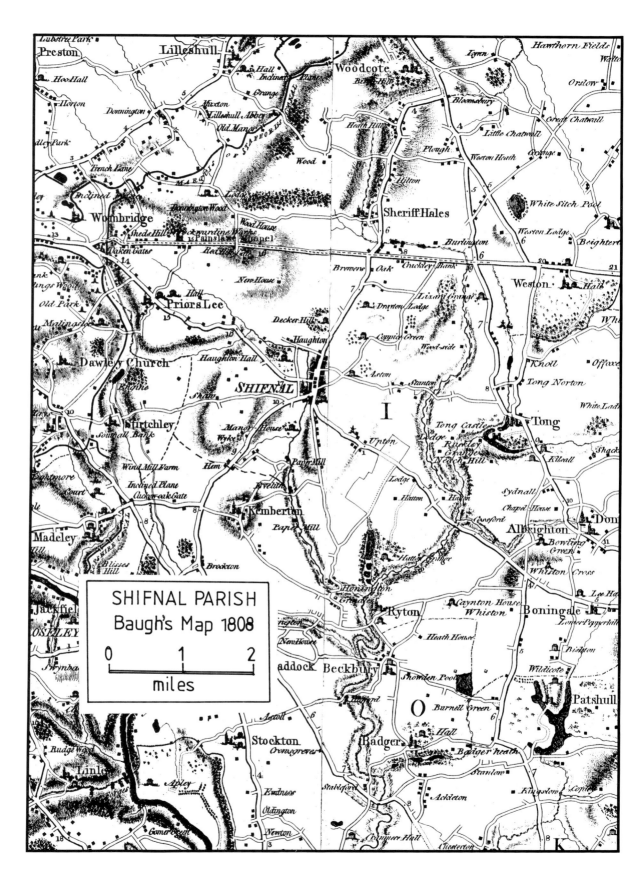

SHIFNAL PARISH
Baugh's Map 1808

0   1   2
miles

view of frankpledge also persisted into the 18th century, and infrequently, even into the nineteenth.

Until the late 17th century most of the population of Shifnal town as well as of the surrounding hamlets were involved in agriculture, even craftsmen such as blacksmiths and weavers, and tradesmen such as innkeepers also had their own cattle and grew some corn. Recent research on probate inventories that listed the possessions of a person just after his death has shown that the bulk of most people's wealth was tied up in stock and crops; household possessions in the early 16th century were very sparse. However during the 16th century Shifnal shared in the general trend of increasing domestic comfort; windows were glazed, chimneys were added, furniture, especially beds, became more plentiful and comfortable and some people accumulated large stocks of household linen.

The probate inventories also show that in the late 17th and the 18th centuries there was a great expansion in the number and range of craftsmen active in the town. There were craftsmen to meet almost all the needs of the local population – tailors, weavers, dyers, skinners, tanners, curriers, shoemakers, saddlers, masons, thatchers and brickmakers. The range of crafts to be found was typical of most small market towns, and many of the crafts persisted until the present century, as some of the photographs show. In Shifnal as in most market towns, mercers, the earliest retailers, handled most of the goods which the farmers of the immediate surroundings could not supply or the craftsmen of the town process.

The group of trades using leather formed the largest group of crafts in the early 18th century, and they were still the largest group at the time of the 1851 census, but Shifnal had no specialist trades to compare with the dominant woollen industry in East Anglia or the Cotswolds, or the iron and coal industries of the nearby Ironbridge Gorge. The farming of the surrounding area was also mixed, as indeed it still is. In the 17th century farmers in many areas began to specialise as agriculture became a matter for commercial enterprise as well as subsistence, but in the Shifnal area most farmers had cattle, sheep, some pigs and poultry and some corn. The components of the corn crop have changed: in the Middle Ages and up to about the 1680s rye and barley were the dominant crops, but in the 18th century rye was superseded by wheat. Though there was no real specialisation, the emphasis in the different elements of farming varied to some extent in the different areas of the parish. Priorslee and Woodhouses in the west of the parish shared the characteristics of the cattle-rearing and cheese-making economy of the Cheshire plain, while the lighter soils of Drayton, Upton and Hatton supported more sheep and corn.

The organisation of farming around Shifnal kept its medieval character late. The open fields around Shifnal town which tenants of Drayton, Haughton, Wyke and the town itself had farmed since the Middle Ages remained in existence until 1793. This is an unusually late date for Shropshire, which by the end of the 16th century was regarded by parliamentary commissioners as a largely enclosed county; only seven Shropshire communities retained their open fields until the age of parliamentary enclosure. However, by the 18th century the medieval pattern of many farmers each working a few scattered strips had changed to one of a few farmers leasing most of the land and paying labourers to work it.

The open fields were only one element in a pattern of land utilization which was very complex, and had been so since the Middle Ages. As well as the large open arable fields (amounting to about 800 acres at the time of enclosure), there were many ancient enclosed fields, both arable and pasture. There were isolated farmsteads as well as hamlets. Some of the hamlets – Hatton, Stanton and Upton – had their own open fields until the early

18th century; others such as Priorslee and Woodhouses, which were later established, had enclosed their open fields early, if indeed they ever had them.

Compared with a parish such as Wigston in Leicestershire where all available land was settled and exploited in the Middle Ages, Shifnal had large areas of common or waste land which remained until the late 18th century, and a manor survey of 1720 could still refer to new intakes of land, meaning land enclosed from the common. Lizard Common covered an area of about 1,000 acres, and though referred to as waste, was in fact very important to the local economy; part of it was intensively coppiced for charcoal making, part was used for grazing sheep and part for pigs. From the late 16th century, as in many areas of Shropshire, smallholders squatted on the fringes of the common, built cottages and enclosed small fields. Another area, Upton Common, of about 450 acres, was heathland until enclosure in 1813. A local historian writing in the 1850s described it as being barren within living memory. This was in great contrast to the similarly light soils of the lands of the manor of Hatton. Hatton belonged to the Cistercian monks of Buildwas Abbey from the early 13th century until the Dissolution, and the monks had much improved their land.

This varied pattern of land utilization was complicated further by small-scale industry. A very early blast furnace was established in 1564 in the lord of the manor's park, and associated forges were situated on the stream bordering Lizard Common. Iron was brought from Snedshill on the western edge of the parish, and charcoal was made in the coppices of the nearby common. By the end of the 17th century the western edge of the parish became increasingly exploited for iron and coal mining, and for about 30 years there was a glasshouse producing bottles and window glass at Snedshill. The parish registers at the beginning of the 18th century show that small squatter settlements on the western edge of the parish were growing rapidly and were composed almost entirely of coalminers. From 1759 Patchers Mill on the stream below the manor house was converted to paper-making. Later the Manor Mill and Hem Mill were also used for a while for paper-making. All this industry, however, remained small-scale. Despite the proximity of the Coalbrookdale coal field, only small areas to the west of the parish shared in its development. *Pigots Directory* of 1829 described Shifnal as being without manufacturing except paper-making; its economy remained basically agricultural.

At the end of the 18th century and beginning of the 19th Shifnal enjoyed a brief spell of prosperity, catering for coaching traffic. The road to Shrewsbury was turnpiked early, in 1726, as part of the route from London to Shrewsbury, and Shrewsbury Road was built to make an easier route through the town than Church Street. There was a regular stagecoach service through the town from 1681, but it was in 1785 when the Irish mail coaches began to pass through Shifnal en route from London to Holyhead that transport became important to the local economy. At the beginning of the 19th century the Holyhead mail coach could do the journey form London to Shifnal in 27 hours. In 1831, after Thomas Telford's improvements to the Holyhead Road, the journey time was reduced to 16½ hours, using 150 horses along the route. Two Shifnal inns, the *Jerningham Arms* and the *Star*, competed in catering for the lucrative trade brought by the coaches. In 1829, 18 coaches a day, including the Holyhead Royal Mail coaches, stopped at Shifnal inns to change horses and pick up and set down passengers. Their arrivals and departures went on throughout the day from the 6.30 a.m. coach to London until midnight when there were two coaches to London and another to Holyhead. It seems that this traffic may have been in decline before the railway to Shifnal was open. In 1844 there were only nine coaches a day scheduled to stop in Shifnal, though the trade appears to have been spread across more inns. The *Jerningham Arms* still serviced most of the coaches, but the *Lion* and the *Wonder* shared this trade as well as the *Star*.

In 1849 the railway from Wolverhampton to Shrewsbury was opened, and the coaching trade quickly dwindled away. The railway passes Shifnal on an impressive viaduct which must have totally changed the visual appearance of the town, even though it was so skilfully engineered that only one building is said to have been demolished to accommodate it. The railway crossed the market square on a handsome iron bridge; it still crosses the square but, since 1953, on a much less handsome bridge. Despite the visual dominance of the railway, it brought no prosperity to Shifnal. The weekly market became of less importance as farmers could reach more distant but larger markets. Today the railway makes Shifnal popular with commuters. The local historian John Randall writing in 1879 contrasted Shifnal before and after the coming of the railway: 'prior to 1849' it was a 'lively little town with a stream of gay stagecoaches with which mingled the royal mail running through it'. After the building of the railway it was a 'quiet little town, respectable in appearance, but producing the impression that it had seen better days, and with its channel of traffic, like that of an old but deviated stream, dried up'. As well as catering for passenger traffic and the long-distance mail coaches, Shifnal was a post town from which rural postmen, mounted letter carriers and carts distributed mail as far afield as Broseley, Much Wenlock and Bridgnorth, but that traffic too was much reduced.

By 1868 Shifnal's trade was described in directories as being supported by its own inhabitants and the 'custom of the gentry'. In other words, Shifnal had reverted to its earlier character of a small market town serving only local needs. The phrase 'custom of the gentry' does, however, hint at some change. Where the hamlets surrounding Shifnal town had earlier been communities of husbandmen and yeomen farmers, by the mid-19th century many of these hamlets had a substantial house belonging to the gentry and a few labourers' cottages. Such estates were mainly built up round a nucleus of what had long been freehold land. For instance, Hatton has had a long history as a distinct entity. Although within Shifnal parish, it was a separate small manor at the time of Domesday. In the early 13th century it was given to Buildwas Abbey as mentioned earlier, and stayed in their hands until the Dissolution. During the 17th century the Slaney family gradually acquired more and more of the estate, and their descendants have been there ever since. In 1764 Plowden Slaney built a handsome brick house designed by Thomas Farnolls Pritchard, later the designer of the bridge at Ironbridge. Part of the grounds are landscaped pools which were once the fishponds of the monks.

The hamlet of Aston lost its identity as a community of husbandmen sometime during the 16th or early 17th century. The rents from Aston tenants were given in 1410 by Henry IV to Battlefield Abbey, a college of chantry priests which he founded in thanksgiving for his victory at the Battle of Shrewsbury in 1403. After the Dissolution Aston came into possession of the Jobber family, and at some point between the levying of the Lay Subsidy of 1524, when there were eight taxpayers in Aston, and the Hearth Tax of 1662, Aston disappeared as a hamlet. The area was emparked, and the Jobbers built a house which the present house replaced in the early 19th century.

The hamlet of Haughton is now largely swallowed up by the spread of new housing from Shifnal town. The 18th and early 19th-century house in its park that belonged to the Brooke family is now the most obvious reminder of the former township. Although Haughton was one of the larger hamlets with several yeomen households, the core of the Haughton Hall estate was freehold land of special significance as long ago as the 12th century when Walter de Dunstanville I, lord of the manor, gave his harpist, Oliver, land at Haughton. His descendants retained Haughton for several generations, and eventually at the beginning of the 16th century it passed by marriage from the Charlton family to the Moretons. From an enquiry into enclosure in 1517, it seems that Robert Moreton of Haughton was responsible for enclosing land at Trillardine. This had been one of the smaller hamlets of the parish in the Middle Ages, and this was the last to be heard of it other than as a field name. The Moretons and their descendants the Brigges and later Brookes gradually acquired more land in the parish, in Drayton and Upton as well as in Haughton. They also leased mills, and in the 17th and 18th centuries they leased the forges at Lizard. In 1575 Richard Moreton bought the advowson and the right to the great tithes from Queen Elizabeth and, in the absence of a resident lord of the manor, the family appears to have assumed the role of squire.

The hamlet of Drayton has almost disappeared. There are a few council houses, a substantial farmhouse, Drayton Lodge, and another large house, Decker Hill. This was rebuilt in about 1810 by the iron-master William Botfield.

This growth of the houses of the gentry around Shifnal in the 18th and 19th centuries was parallelled by the decline of the manor house. The earliest manor house is believed to have been a moated homestead near the church. The site was excavated in 1962 before the building of a new estate, and the findings suggested that this house went out of use in the mid-14th century, The present manor house was probably (though not definitely, its history is very obscure) built at the end of the 14th century and much altered since. A drawing of the house on an early map of 1635 shows a partly half-timbered house around a courtyard with a new wing with large windows in the late Elizabethan style. The gardens were laid out as a fashionable pleasure ground with a summerhouse, and there was a large orchard nearby. An inventory of the contents of the manor house in 1634 gives a vivid impression of the luxurious furnishings of the many rooms at that date. A few years previously Lady Ann Dacre, mother of Thomas Howard, Earl of Arundel, who was then lord of the manor in the right of his wife Lady Alathea Talbot, had spent her last years there, but after that the manor house seems never to have been used as a manorial home again. Since then it has been leased as a farmhouse, subdivided into flats, and partially destroyed by fire. The surrounding land still belongs to the descendants of the Talbots and Howards, but their main seat has always been elsewhere. As well as this ring of large houses around Shifnal a feature of the present landscape is the large number of substantial brick farmhouses standing alone amongst their fields and dating from the end of the 18th century and the beginning of the 19th, after the enclosure of the open fields.

During the second half of the 19th century Shifnal gradually recovered from the loss of the transport trade; only the establishment of the chainworks of Messrs. Edge near the railway at Upton in 1870 was, however, of more than local significance. They were the inventors of a type of flat chain much used before the invention of wire ropes. The directories of the 1860s list trades that for the most part are the same as those recorded in the parish registers of the early 18th century. Among the few new trades were clock and watchmakers, insurance agents, veterinary surgeons, painters, coal merchants, hairdressers, solicitors and bankers.

In the second half of the 19th century Shifnal was described as being chiefly one street with several minor streets off it; the houses were irregularly built, and many of the cottages were of mean appearance. There were, however, said to be several good inns and private residences and respectable shops in most branches of the retail trade. The market was still held weekly, though it was less important than formerly. The population grew only slowly during the 19th century. In 1821, when the coaching boom was at its height, the population of the whole parish was 4,411, in 1851 it was 5,616 and in 1891 it was 6,615. Much of this increase had occurred in the west of the parish, in the flourishing industrial areas of Snedshill and Priorslee.

As it became more populous the Priorslee area acquired its own shops, Methodist chapel and school; its chapel of ease was rebuilt in 1836, and 1863 became an independent church. In 1898 Priorslee finally became a separate settlement and civil parish. In 1901 at the next census, the population of Priorslee was 2,930, and that of Shifnal 3,321. In fact the Priorslee area was then at the height of its prosperity. The Lilleshall Company at Snedshill had extensive iron, coal and fire-clay mines, blast furnaces and steel works, foundries, forges, rolling mills and brickworks. In 1902 Priorslee and Snedshill were described as wastes of slag and cinder heaps, some a century old, others still smoking, and full of great iron furnaces most impressive at night. In 1911 the population went up to 3,017, but in 1921 and 1931 it declined. Now the coal and iron mines have all closed; the Lilleshall Company still operates, though as a smaller organisation specialising in steel. Much of the company's land has been taken over by Telford Development Corporation, and the area is now part of Telford.

During the 19th century Shifnal acquired many of the institutions typical of the time. In 1849 a Mechanical Institute opened and offered lectures, a library and reading rooms. These institutes were set up in many towns and met with varying degrees of success, but Shifnal's seems to have had a long and active life. From about 1840 there was a National School with about 150 children. In 1854 it was moved to new buildings at the Innage. There had been a small grammar school since 1595, but it had always been rather meagrely endowed. Around 1880 it lost control of even these endowments and after unsuccessful legal struggles it had to close down. Chapels for dissenters were established. There were two Baptist chapels, one in Aston Street and one in Shrewsbury Road, but in the 1870s the small Aston Street chapel closed. There were also Primitive and Wesleyan Methodists; in 1880 the Wesleyan Methodists built a large new chapel in Victoria Road. In 1860 Lord Stafford, lord of the manor, paid for a Roman Catholic church and school on his land in Shrewsbury Road. Many of these buildings can be seen in the following photographs.

One of the most striking developments in 19th-century Shifnal, in common with most towns, was the proliferation of public officials and their offices, and in fact of a whole variety of buildings serving the community. In 1817 the group of parishes in the Shifnal Union built a workhouse which was extended in 1840 to accommodate 150 people. A magistrates' building was put up in 1840, and in 1850 a lock-up and a constable's house were added. There was a stamp office in the Market Place, and an excise office at the *Bell Inn*. In 1847 a gas works began operating in the High Street, and the streets were lit by gas. In 1868 a Market Hall with large public rooms was opened and remained popular for many years for social functions such as dances. The local Volunteer Battalion of the King's Shropshire Light Infantry also met there. In 1902 in his book describing places along the Holyhead Road, C.G. Harper described Shifnal as 'a little place, changed less in the course of three hundred years than any along this road'. Until the 1960s Shifnal changed very little. It remained a small market town with even its market in decline. Early in the century the weekly market ceased and a cattle market only was held on alternate Mondays; in the 1960s this stopped as well. Between 1921 and 1931 the population actually fell. In 1934 another area at the western end of the parish was removed, this time to the parish and urban district of Oakengates. The workhouse was no longer administered by the Shifnal Union but by the Wenlock Area Guardians Committee sitting in Madeley. The impression is one of stagnation if not actual decay. The 1968 *Shropshire Directory* said that Shifnal at present has no historical or architectural features to attract the visitor, and it predicted that there were signs of building and industrial development which would greatly alter its character.

In fact neither of these judgements is totally accurate. It is true that many of the old buildings to be seen in the photographs, especially the timber buildings, have been demolished, particularly in the 1960s. This has left large gaps in the main streets which have only gradually been filled over the last 20 years. The Cheapside and Bradford Street area where the market would have been held in the Middle Ages was filled in with crowded buildings over the centuries. Now with the buildings cleared and a weekly market re-established, it has returned to the open market place of the Middle Ages. However, there are still groups of half-timbered buildings in the West Midlands style, and the church is beautiful and of considerable interest. Due to a serious fire in 1591 Shifnal had no buildings of an earlier date other than the church, Old Idsall House and a mysterious and unidentified length of medieval sandstone wall near the shopping centre. As well as the remaining 17th-century half-timbered houses there are attractive brick houses of the 18th and 19th centuries.

The prediction of great change has also not proved wholly accurate. There has been much new building; there are new housing estates around the town centre, on one of the former open fields (the Calverley estate), on former glebe land (Silvermere) and on the former demesne of the lord of the manor (Manor Park). The population has doubled since the 1930s, and most of the inhabitants are now newcomers, many of them working outside Shifnal. Yet this influx of people and spread of building has not greatly changed Shifnal's essential character. There is some light industry, but not enough to be overwhelming. Shifnal's hinterland is still rural, even though only a small proportion of the population now works on the land. The decline of the town has been arrested and it enjoys a modest prosperity. Though not as obviously appealing to tourists as Ludlow or Shrewsbury, Shifnal has had a long history as a community and much of its past can still be traced in the modern town. In spite of the new estates, the basic plan of Shifnal's main streets still reaveals its early history. The bridge over the stream and the area around the church is the oldest part of the settlement and was once known as Idsall, while the long wide street known as Park Street, Cheapside, Broadway and High Street at different parts of its length is still an obvious example of a 13th-century planned market town. Off this main street the long medieval burgages or building plots are still apparent in a few places. Shifnal and its surrounding hamlets are, to use W.G. Hoskins' much-quoted analogy, a palimpsest where many strands of historical development are superimposed and interwoven.

The Plates

.

Buildings and Streets

1. St Andrew's parish church. Shifnal has a large and imposing church built of red sandstone and in various architectural styles from Norman to Perpendicular. The graveyard, once known as Dawley bury-yard, is also exceptionally large. Since 1905, when this photograph was taken, many of the old gravestones have been moved to a memorial garden.

2.   The exterior of the church from the south in 1788. As many as two-thirds of Shropshire churches were restored by the Victorians to fit in with their conception of a Gothic church. Classical features were removed, and some churches that appeared to be too agricultural or domestic in character were given Gothic windows. Shifnal seems to be an essentially medieval church, repaired rather than restored.

3.   From its large graveyard and the fact that the church was cruciform from an early date, it seems that Shifnal was a minster or mother church in Anglo-Saxon times. The oldest work to be seen today, however, is Norman, including these windows in the north wall of the chancel.

4. This picture looks down the church towards the east window with its unusual tracery dating from about 1300. The exact date of the picture is unknown, but it must have been taken before the restoration of the church which was completed in 1879. During this restoration the box pews were replaced and the pulpit moved to the other side of the church.

5. The chancel has a fine Elizabethan hammerbeam roof which was probably built after a serious fire in 1591. Since this picture was drawn in about 1895, the tombs of the Brigges family, here shown near the altar, have been moved to the Lady Chapel or Moreton Chapel, which adjoins the chancel on the south side and was then used as a vestry and storeroom.

6. This carving is in shadow above the Norman chancel arch. The pagan symbol of the green man can be traced back to the fourth century, though most English examples are of 13th-century date. The Shifnal green man is unusual in being a side view and in having a cornucopia.

7. The west window is late Early English in style and dates from about 1270, though it has several times needed extensive repair. In this picture the unusual double set of crossing arches can be seen. It is supposed that the Norman arches supported a tower which fell, and stronger arches were built for the new tower in about 1300.

8. This mid-19th-century drawing shows the interior of the church before restoration. The 13th-century porch continues inside the church into the south aisle, and there is a room above known as the parvise. On the right can be seen one of the galleries added in the late 17th century and removed during the restoration.

9. This picture, looking east in 1895, shows the reredos dedicated in that year, the brass gas light fittings and the pews which replaced the box pews.

10. This external tomb recess on the south wall of the chancel is a most unusual feature. There are similar tombs on the south side of Lichfield Cathedral and just a very few elsewhere in the Lichfield diocese. Probably only someone involved in rebuilding would have been able to have his tomb incorporated in the fabric of the building in this way.

11.   The vicarage garden in about 1905. Glebe terriers which described church property for the Bishop of Lichfield show that pleasure grounds with flower beds were laid out in 1841. Before that the vicarage was surrounded with the usual outbuildings of a working farm – barns, stables and foldyards.

12.   The north front of the vicarage in the early years of this century. This building replaced an earlier vicarage in 1775. The glebe terrier of 1779 described it as having a 'vestibule with two large parlours in front with a hall, kitchen, two pantries and a scullery backwards'.

13. The church and vicarage in 1898 from a meadow once known as Bowling Alley Piece. The meadow was originally part of the lord of the manor's park, a deer park from the 13th to the 17th century.

14. This verger's cottage which stood on glebe land opposite the church has been recently demolished. The cottage was of early 19th-century date, but it replaced a late 17th-century cottage built for the parish clerk.

15. The Wesleyan chapel, known as the Trinity Methodist church in Victoria Road. It was built in 1880 to replace an earlier chapel in Cheapside. Methodism must have been flourishing in Shifnal at that time as this earlier chapel was reported as having a large Sunday school and evening services that were crowded out. There were also Primitive Methodists who had a small chapel at the northern end of the town.

16. An interior view of St Mary's Roman Catholic church in Shrewsbury Road. It was built in 1860 at the expense of Lord Stafford, the lord of the manor. Lord Stafford presented the church with a pre-Reformation chalice which was found in a Yorkshire shop, and was inscribed with the words 'Restore mee to Sheafnal in Shropshire'.

17. Shifnal manor house in a picture taken before 1905. The house stands well outside the town surrounded by fields which were once a deer park. The part of the house in the foreground was destroyed by fire in 1974. In the early 17th century this part of the garden was laid out with flowerbeds in the formal patterns then fashionable.

18. A late 18th-century painting of the manor house. From an early (1635) illustrated map it is known that the summerhouse (still standing today) was in existence in the early 17th century, though the exact date of its building is not known. A letter to the Earl of Shrewsbury in the 1590s describes the difficulty of building the window on the right because of the steep slope.

19.   The manor house and outbuildings from the south-west. The house was built about 1400, though it has been much added to and altered. It stands on a well defended site, and this picture gives some indication of the steep banks still surrounding it.

20.   The Manor Pool. Left of the Mill Cottage near the pool was a mill finally dismantled in the 1960s. Behind the tall trees in the centre of the picture was a very early blast furnace which was in operation from 1564 until the early years of the 17th century. The pool was known as the Furnace Pool as late as the end of the 18th century. It was very popular with fishermen and skaters until it was drained in the 1960s. Attempts to drain it and divert the feeder streams have not been completely successful because of persistent springs.

21. Deckerhill Hall. William Botfield, iron-master, built this house on the site of an earlier one in the mid-19th century. The Botfields owned many iron furnaces and coal mines in the area which is now Telford. The grounds are now a golf course, and the house is the club house.

22. The conservatory at Deckerhill Hall in 1898. Beriah Botfield, M.P., had the gardens lavishly laid out with ornamental flower beds, conservatories and hothouses. A 1910 sale catalogue described this conservatory as having a revolving stand in the middle.

23.   Hatton Grange. Although within Shifnal parish, Hatton was a separate manor and was owned by Buildwas Abbey in the Middle Ages. Since the end of the 17th century it has been owned by the Slaney family whose members have for many generations served as M.P.s and J.P.s. Plowden Slaney built the present house in 1764, the architect being Thomas Farnolls Pritchard, designer of the first iron bridge.

24.   Hatton Grange in 1898. Many of the bricks used in the house were made on the estate, but those on the three main fronts of the house were made three miles away at Albrighton which was said to be 'famous for this material', a justifiable claim in view of the well preserved state of the brickwork.

25. Haughton Hall, *c.*1910. In the absence of a resident lord of the manor, the Charltons and their descendants the Moretons, Brigges and Brookes who lived in the Hall acted as lords from the Middle Ages until modern times. The present house dates partly from the early 18th and partly from the early 19th century.

26. The north front of Haughton Hall in 1898. The main entrance is on this side. The south front looks across parkland which was once one of the open arable fields of Shifnal. As well as the park there were pleasure grounds, conservatories and hothouses in the 19th century.

27. Haughton Grange in the early years of this century. The pool (which had powered a mill since the 12th century) was drained in the 1930s. Until the Dissolution the mill belonged to Wombridge Priory. This mill cottage is over 400 years old. The mill itself was burned down in 1913 and never rebuilt.

28. Evelith Manor. The present house is a mid-19th-century building. After his defeat at the Battle of Worcester in 1651 Prince Charles (later Charles II) was passing the nearby Evelith Mill on his way to attempt to cross the River Severn at Madeley and escape into Wales, when the miller challenged him, and he was forced to run and hide in a hedge.

29. The National School, later the Church of England School, at the Innage in 1910. The school was built in 1854 at the expense of the Brooke family of Haughton Hall and other landowners. It was built to replace an earlier school on the site of a house (Inglewood) nearer the church. On the left of the picture was an area once known as the Green.

30. The old school was deserted in 1969, but its bell was taken to the new St Andrew's School. The old school was demolished in the 1970s and a new housing estate now covers the area. This old school was the descendant of an Elizabethan grammar school which was rather small and poorly endowed. By the 18th century it had split into an English and a classical school. The English school became affiliated to the National Society in 1816 and kept most of the endowments.

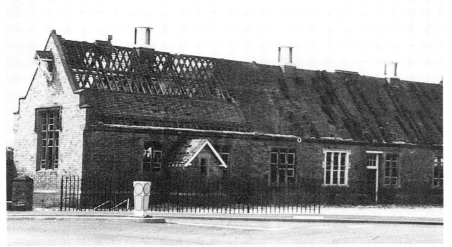

31. The old school house was occupied by the headmaster of the school until 1969. It was also demolished in the mid-1970s.

32. Church Street around 1905. This is the older part of the town, once known as Idsall. The white house at the end near the church steps, Old Idsall House, is supposed to be the oldest house in Shifnal. It survived the fire of 1591, when at least 30 houses were destroyed and the church roof was also burnt.

33. This picture was taken from the top of Church Street looking towards the station entrance in the mid-1960s. The Station House was built in 1849 in pale yellow brick in an Italianate style and demolished in the late 1960s.

34. The east side of the Square or Market Place in 1905 looking south towards Park Street. The old building on the right was dismantled in 1936, all its timbers numbered and re-erected at Castlecroft, Wolverhampton.

35. The other side of the Market Place in about 1900. T.C. Smith, saddler, later transferred his business across the road to the shop with the awning in the previous picture. The business lasted from about 1895 until the Second World War.

36. The Market Place in 1905. The building on the left with the balcony on the roof became a public house, the *Star*, in 1813, and vied with the *Jerningham Arms* in catering for the coaching trade. Dr. Thomas Percy found there the old verses which he published in 1768 as *Reliques of Ancient English Poetry*.

37. The Market Place looking up Bradford Street in the 1920s. The railway was brought through Shifnal on a viaduct cutting the town in two, and it was carried over the market place by this handsome bridge cast by Horseley Ironworks, Tipton, in 1848. The railway connecting Wolverhampton with Shrewsbury opened on 12 November 1849.

38. The east side of Park Street in 1905 looking north toward the Market Place. The *Unicorn Inn* on the right was nick-named the *Fork and Basket* because the Irish labourers who came over to work on the harvest left their tools there. This part of Park Street near the Market Place was known as Horsefair until the 1890s.

39. The west side of Park Street also in about 1905. The inn, the *King's Head*, was demolished in about 1940. The other half-timbered buildings are now also gone and the area is a car park.

40. The east side of Park Street in 1905. The building with the curved front has belonged to Lloyds Bank since about 1874. For about 25 years before that it belonged to the Shropshire Banking Company. The railings were removed during the 1939-45 war.

41. The *Jerningham Arms* on the west side of Park Street, pictured here in the 1930s, was built in 1706 and was very busy during the stage coach boom in Shifnal around 1800. Eighteen coaches a day passed through Shifnal, most calling at the *Jerningham Arms*, though there was competition from the *Star* and some of the other inns. Jerningham was the family name of the lords of the manor from 1762 until 1913.

42. Idsall House in Park Street. The house, dated 1699, is described by Nikolaus Pevsner as a good example of the William and Mary style. It was probably the first brick building in the town. For much of this century and the last the house was home to Shifnal's doctor. It is now part of a hotel.

43.   The old cottage hospital in Park Street. This picture was taken in 1898 when the hospital was new. It was a very small hospital with only 10 to 15 beds. During the Second World War it was a Land Army hostel.

44.   The Shifnal Union Workhouse nicknamed the 'Spike'. The workhouse was built in 1817 and extended in 1840 to serve an area of 67 square miles, including Albrighton, Tong and Sheriffhales as well as Shifnal. It could accommodate 150, though there were usually about 60 inmates. The 'interior arrangements' were 'well contrived for the comfort, convenience and cleanliness of the inmates'.

45.   The new voluntary cottage hospital was built on land given by Mr. B. Hough of Lodge Hill Farm and opened by Lady Bradford of Weston Park in 1939. The hospital expanded to include the old workhouse buildings, but has recently contracted again, and the workhouse has been converted into retirement flats.

46. The toll house, formerly on the corner of Park Lane and the Wolverhampton road. The Wolverhampton to Shrewsbury road was turnpiked early, in 1726, but the toll house was built later, in about 1825, when Thomas Telford improved the road as part of the route to Holyhead. Telford himself designed the toll houses along the Holyhead road. He designed four types, this two-storey type being the least common. A living room, kitchen and toll room were provided downstairs and two bedrooms upstairs. The toll gates were removed in 1886. The toll house was used as a petrol station in the 1930s, and was demolished accidentally by a lorry during the Second World War.

47. An old cottage, now demolished, which stood in a hollow beside Park Lane. The Park Lane area was settled by cottagers squatting on the lord of the manor's land at the end of the 17th century.

48. Looking along Victoria Road around 1950. This road was part of Thomas Telford's improvements to the route to Holyhead, and was known until Queen Victoria's Diamond Jubilee as New Street. The garage has been replaced by a new building but is still a garage.

49. Further down Victoria Road showing Trinity Methodist church. The house on the right which belonged to Dr. L'Oste Brown has been replaced by a block of flats. The styles of the buildings show that although the road was opened in the 1820s, it was only built up slowly.

50. Bradford Street in 1900. At this date and until about 1917 the *British Workman* was a temperance hotel, sometimes described as a coffee tavern; earlier it had been a library and free reading room given by Mr. and Mrs. H. MacLean of Aston Hall. The building with the tower was the Market Hall, known locally as the Town Hall, built in 1868. It was used as the drill hall of the Territorial Battalion of the King's Shropshire Light Infantry before 1914, and for dances and concerts until after the Second World War.

51. This pre-1905 photograph of Bradford Street looking north shows the *Talbot Hotel* next to the Market Hall and old cottages beyond. The *Talbot* was named after the Earls of Shrewsbury who held Shifnal manor from 1422 until 1616. All the buildings on the left were infilling of the medieval market place, and all are now gone.

52.   These two shops on the east side of Bradford Street were originally one building together with the house on the left. It was a farm until opened as shops by Mr. Cheadle in the 1880s. The left-hand shop was a watchmaker's, and remained so until recently. The right-hand shop has changed many times, but for 30 years from 1954 it was well known as Mrs. Spencer's sweet shop. The building is 17th-century but has blackened timbers which may have been re-used after the fire of 1591.

53. King's Yard was a narrow lane of old cottages stretching back from the main street towards the Wesley Brook. Cattle from the farm in Bradford Street (*see opposite*) were led down this lane to drink at the brook. The cottages were demolished in the 1970s.

54. This picture was taken in the 1950s from the Broadway looking south down Bradford Street. For about 30 years before its demolition in 1972 the building on the right was used by the Registrar for Births, Marriages and Deaths. The *Crown Inn* was renowned for cock-fighting at the end of the 18th century.

55. The Broadway in the 1920s looking north. The half-timbered cottage on the left (now demolished) belonged at one time to Mr. Fullerton, horsebreaker. He looked after the horse which pulled the fire engine, and the horse is said to have recognised the sound of the fire alarm.

56. Looking north along the Broadway in about 1913. Until the 1890s High Street, the Broadway and Bradford Street were all known as High Street. This wide street is a continuation of the market area, but unlike Bradford Street and Cheapside it only had one or two buildings erected in the centre.

57. The old court house was built in 1840, and a police constable's house with lock-up was added in 1850. The building was scheduled for demolition in 1947, but the county council library committee thought it would be useful as a library for the remaining 18 months of the lease – it was a library until 1972. The children's section of the library occupied the magistrate's raised dais.

58. These old cottages on the west side of the Broadway leading from Cheapside have now been demolished. The Spencer Court flats now occupy the site, the name recalling the former Spencer's smithy (see 84).

59. A typical Shifnal scene. Much of the demolition of buildings in Shifnal such as that of this house in the Broadway has puzzled local inhabitants; the house was substantial and apparently sound. There was little pressure on land, and after many years the space is still empty and used as a car park.

60.   Old houses in the High Street. They were lived in until the 1920s, but Shifnal's first council houses now occupy the site.

61.   The *White Hart* public house on the east side of the High Street, which is the northerly continuation of the Broadway. Shifnal has long been known for the large number of inns per head of the population. The half-timbered cottages survived into the 1930s.

62.   One of the many half-timbered cottages which formerly stood in Shifnal. This one was in the Broadway. This style lingered late in Shifnal, especially for smaller houses. As brick became a more popular building material cottages such as this were given brick infill panels between the timbers. After the cottage was demolished the site was a coal yard for a while, and now sheltered homes for the elderly have been built.

63.   Aston Street looking east in about 1913. The *Anvil* public house on the right was opened in 1856. Leather processing was once important in the town, and in the 17th and 18th centuries this street was known as Cordwainers Lane. Since its development in the early 17th century the street seems always to have been mainly an area of labourers' cottages.

64. Shrewsbury Road in 1905 looking east. This road was made to avoid Church Street when the route to Shrewsbury was turnpiked in 1726, and was superseded in turn by Thomas Telford's improvements. The road was called Old Salop (Shrewsbury) Road to distinguish it from New Street (Victoria Road). The building in the middle distance was a steam mill which ceased operating in about 1900, and was later used as a brewery.

65. The Innage Farm next to the old school. This picture was taken in the 1960s. It remained a working farm into the 1970s, but the Idsall Green housing estate now occupies the site.

66. Haughton Lane looking very rural in the 1920s. The area on the left is part of Haughton Hall park, and it is still open land.

67. Haughton Lane looking north, showing the houses built on the east side in the 1930s. In the foreground on the right was the field known as the May Field, used for the annual maypole dancing.

68. The bridge over the Wesley Brook at the end of Haughton Lane in the 1930s. This small stream was very important to the inhabitants of Haughton and Shifnal. For instance, as well as the obvious harnessing of water power to work mills, in the 17th century the water was used for soaking hemp and flax, even though this was an offence punishable by the manor court.

69. Priorslee Chapel in a drawing of 1788. Wombridge Priory built up an estate in Priorslee in the 12th century, and this chapel is associated with the priory. It survived to serve the area's growing industrial population in the 18th century, though it was said to have only a few services inconveniently timed, and therefore little attended. It was replaced by a new church in 1836 and the building was demolished in 1838.

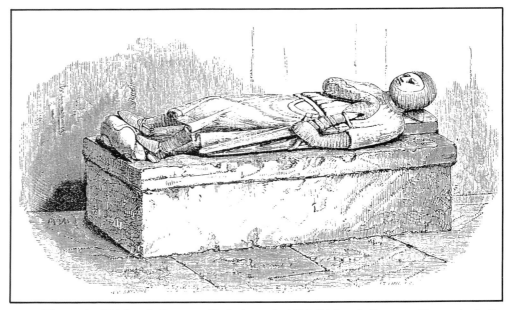

70. The tomb of Walter de Dunstanville I, drawn in 1855. Walter de Dunstanville was lord of the manor of Shifnal (and land in Wiltshire and Normandy as well) from about 1155 to 1195. He spent much of his life in Normandy, but is thought to have retired to Wombridge Priory, of which he was one of the main benefactors, and died there. His tomb is now in Shrewsbury Abbey.

71. This picture of the 1780s appears to have been drawn from a viewpoint to the south-west of the church just along the Bridgnorth road, but there is now no trace of any of the other buildings in the picture, nor of the strange structure which appears to be on the church roof. There is no evidence now of the pool in the foreground. The picture is full of puzzles; perhaps it owes something to artistic licence.

Shifnal at Work

72. This chemist's shop was situated where Barclays Bank is now from about 1926 to 1934. Mr. Murray is standing with his assistant, Miss Lucy Beamand.

73. Fenn's shoe shop in 1924 in the Market Place with the manageress, Miss Gwen Dean. The shop was later known as the Globe Shoe Stores. Fenn's business was an old one; it had traded on this site since about 1879, and for about 30 years before that in the High Street. Originally they made the boots and shoes offered for sale.

74. Miss Gertrude Clarke outside Hughes' Dairy in Bradford Street. This dairying business, which was based at Admirals Farm on the Newport Road, continued until the Second World War. They made deliveries with churns from which customers' jugs were filled with milk. Hughes also ran a coal factor's business at the station.

75. Payton's bakery and confectionery in Church Street in 1919. This shop was in business from about 1913 until 1930.

76. Miss Hitchen's shop in the Market Place in 1922. This shop sold drapery, ladies' underwear and fancy goods, and was in business from about 1913 to 1922.

77. Adams' fruit shop in Cheapside in the 1930s. Cheapside was the narrow street to the west of the in-filled market area. Adams moved to the Broadway during the Second World War.

78. J.C. Lloyd, grocer, in the closing week in 1971. This shop played an important part in Shifnal life for many years, specialising in catering for the gentry in the big houses surrounding the town. The business started in about 1877 in Church Street and moved to Park Street in 1895. They had their own bottling plant at the back of the premises and also cured their own bacon.

79. Training race horses was for a while one of Shifnal's more unusual occupations. This is Cornelius Doyle who worked for J. Reid Walker of Ruckley Grange, a well known trainer. The horses were trained at The Gallops at Stanton. Shifnal had its own race meetings intermittently during the 19th century.

80. Marshall's printing works operated here for about 17 years. The printing works opened in 1910 at the back of their stationery shop in the Market Place. In the following year, as business expanded, they moved to John Street, a narrow lane off the Market Place, until all the buildings in this area were demolished.

81.   Workmen at Williams the wheelwright's and carpenter's before the First World War. John Williams, the owner,
between the shafts. The firm has operated in Aston Street since the 1850s. Near the group of workmen was an old sawpit.

82. A general purpose cart made by Williams. Recent investigation shows that this site was used for wheelwrighting even earlier than the mid-19th century when the Williams' business began.

83. A waggon made by Williams especially for Ilford Rural District Council. Waggons like this continued to be made into the 1930s.

84. Spencer's blacksmith's shop in the Broadway. Blacksmiths had always been important and they often managed to retain their position by taking work servicing cars as they became more common. Spencer's later moved to Church Street, but the premises have now been demolished.

85.   The demolition of the old railway bridge in 1953. Officially the bridge needed replacing because it could no longer get insurance cover; local opinion maintained that it could have lasted another hundred years. Demolition and replacement proved to be a considerably more difficult undertaking than expected.

86.   This view of the men working on the new bridge with Church Street on the left shows clearly the dominating position of the railway in the centre of the town.

87. Lifting gear at Edge & Sons Rope and Chain Works. This firm was established at Coalport in 1795 and moved to Shifnal 75 years later. The founder of the firm, Benjamin Edge, invented a flat-link, wood-keyed pit chain which superseded hemp ropes for winding in pits 50 years before wire ropes were adapted for the purpose.

88. Edge & Sons had their own railway sidings (the main reason for moving to Shifnal) and wires and cables were exported all over the world. The closing of the works was a great loss to Shifnal, and the area was derelict for some years. A small industrial estate now occupies the area and enjoys a modest prosperity; it depends on road transport, however, and the sidings no longer exist.

ESTABLISHED 1800.

EDGE & SONS, LIMITED,

Wire Rope & Chain Manufacturers,

SHIFNAL, SALOP, England.

89. Mr. Green in the 1930s holding woven wire rope; he is wearing a belt of flat wire rope. The chains were tested at Lloyds Proving House at Tipton, Staffordshire. Chains were supplied to the Admiralty throughout the Second World War.

90. This medal was awarded to Edge & Sons at the Philadelphia Exhibition in 1876 for the 'superior make of their chains'. They had earlier received an award at the Crystal Palace Exhibition of 1851. The telephone number of the works was Shifnal 1, which was retained until the closure of the works.

91. Victoria Road and Hall's the printers in the early years of the century. The business of printers, stationers and booksellers began in about 1879, and for many years Daniel Hall combined this business with the office of postmaster. The printing works no longer exist, but the post office still occupies the site.

92. The post office staff in 1955 at the back of the post office in Victoria Road. The postmaster, Mr. R. Turnock, has served on the local council for many years. The occasion of this photograph was the presentation of the safe driving awards. In coaching days Shifnal had been an important postal town, but this traffic to a large extent disappeared with the coming of the railway.

Shifnal People
and Community Life

93. Mrs. Exley outside Park House in Park Street. Donkey carts like this were popular for many years. The Exley family lived in Park House from about 1905 to 1920. The previous owners from about 1870 were the Horton family. In 1854 Samuel Horton bought the Snedshill Iron Furnaces and added them to the Lilleshall Company partnership in 1855. The company rapidly became one of the country's leading manufacturers of wrought iron.

94. The Edge family outside their home, Brooklands. Benjamin Edge, the founder of the firm, was reputed to have come from a Quaker family in Norfolk; his descendants have settled in Shifnal.

95. Mr. Ernest Beamand in his Foresters regalia in about 1900. The photograph was taken in the garden of Mr. Thurtle, a well known photographer who photographed local events for many years.

96. The Martin family in the early years of this century. They were millers who lived and worked at the Manor Mill.

97.   A group of Oddfellows. Like the Foresters, Oddfellows belonged to a friendly society which provided mutual aid against the debts caused by illness, death or old age. These societies grew up in the 17th and 18th centuries but were most numerous in the 19th century.

98.   This old car, a James and Brown of 1900, is thought to have been the first car in Shifnal. It is now in the City and Guilds engineering museum in London. Members of the Spencer family are seated in the car. Blacksmiths were often the most enthusiastic champions of this new form of transport.

99.   An old Alvis belonging to Dr. Kennedy loaded with camping equipment for the Shifnal Rovers and Scouts in 1929.

100.   Charabancs outside the cinema in the Broadway. They were commandeered during the General Strike of 1926.

SHIFNAL PARISH COUNCIL.

FIRE BRIGADE.

SCALE OF CHARGES.

		£	s.	d.
For the use of Engine and appliances if required beyond the limits of the Parish ...		4	4	0
do. Hose Cart		0	10	0
do. Hand Pump		0	10	0
do. Fire Brigade for the first 2 hours a minimum charge of... ...		3	3	0
For each hour after		1	1	0
For Superintendent when Engine is required ...		1	1	0
do. Hand Pump only		0	10	6
do. when neither Engine or Hand Pump are required, for first hour		0	5	0
do. for each hour after		0	3	0
For Horse Hire		3	3	0
Driver of Engine		0	5	0
For use of Hose (per length)		0	5	0
Cleaning Engine, Lamps, &c.		0	12	6
do. Hose Cart		0	2	6
Washing and Drying Hose, per 25 yards length ...		0	1	6

For Damage to Engine and Accoutrements the actual cost.

Time is reckoned from the Receipt of Alarm until the return to the Fire Station.

By Order of the

SHIFNAL PARISH COUNCIL,

BENJ. FARMER,

Clerk to the Council.

30th day of January, 1925.

101. This 1925 scale of charges for calling out the fire brigade is so complicated that considerable accounting skill must have been needed every time the fire brigade was called out. Note that the charge is for horse hire.

102.   The fire engine and crew outside the Shrewsbury Road fire station in the early 1930s. This was Shifnal's first motorised fire engine. The fire brigade had earlier been based at the Town Hall in Bradford Street. Following the reorganisation of the service, the station pictured is now disused, and fire engines are based at Telford.

103.   Shifnal Club Day procession (always the last Saturday in June) in 1909. Since the mid-19th century it had been customary for members of the town's clubs such as the Oddfellows and Foresters to march in procession. The procession was headed by some local worthy carrying a staff bearing a brass dove, the symbol of the Dove Club.

104.   Club Day, 1910. The band was established by Mr. J. Cheadle, the watchmaker in the 1890s. He was an excellent musician and himself provided the uniforms. The band played at concerts and dances and around the streets, especially on Christmas Day. The band room was at the back of the shop where the instruments and uniforms were stored. When Mr. Cheadle died, the funeral cortège was escorted to the church by the band, almost too overcome to play.

105.   The Club Day parade of 1910. The decorated horse and cart was called the wedding. After a lapse during and after the Second World War, a regular carnival procession with floats was revived in 1968 and is still very popular. A funfair takes over the Broadway.

Shifnal Club Day

AND

Hospital Saturday

JUNE 29th, 1912.

All Ladies and Gentlemen interested in the above are respectfully invited to attend a

PARISH MEETING

to be held in the

Lecture Hall

of the

British Workman, Shifnal,

on

Tuesday next, May 21st

at 8 o'clock in the evening to make arrangements for celebrating this important event, to be held this year as usual.

The kind assistance of the Public is much needed and is cordially invited.

Dated this 15th day of May, 1912.

Benj. Farmer,
Clerk to the Shifnal Parish Council.

JAMES LEAKE, Junr.,
Chairman of Parish Council.

Printed and Published by D. Hall, Victoria Printing Works, Shifnal

106. This poster shows that most of the Club Day profits were necessary for the running of the cottage hospital (*see* no. 43). Maintaining even a small hospital evidently involved much community effort.

Shiffnal Fair.

BY Order of Sir WILLIAM JERNINGHAM, BART. Lord of the Manor of Idſal, otherwiſe Shiffnal in the County of Salop; NOTICE is here by given; that,

NO FAIR

will be held or kept in future at Shiffnal on the 5*th* of Auguſt: but that in lieu thereof, one will be annually held in that Town the 27*th* day of March in every Year, except the day falls on a Sunday, and then on the following day.

Likewiſe, that the Fair called the Winter Fair, will in future be held as uſual at that Place, on the 22*nd* of November in every year, except it falls upon a Sunday, and then on the Monday following.

Shiffnal Manor Houſe,
July 3d. 1805.

SCARROTT, PRINTER, SHIFFNAL.

107. The Shifnal fair has a long tradition. The first charter for a market and fair dates from 1245 and further royal charters were obtained in 1315 and 1471. The tolls from fairs were a source of profit for manorial lords, and this poster is interesting in showing that the fair was still a manorial prerogative in the early 19th century.

108. A group of children in Aston Street in the early years of the century. No one seems to remember why the children should have been standing in the road but they make an interesting and charming group.

109. These are the girls in the school in 1912.

110. The schoolgirls in 1923. In 1922 the girls and boys departments were amalgamated. Mr J. Chard, on the right, was the headmaster until 1931.

111.   The infants' department just prior to being transferred to the new Curriers Lane School in 1960. The picture was taken outside what was originally the girls' part of the school.

112.   Mr. W. Morris, headmaster 1931-1958, at his retirement presentation in July 1958. A strict disciplinarian, Mr. Morris was much admired by his staff.

113.   Parents' Day in 1925. The boys were presenting a physical training display on the school lawn which was where the youth club is now.

114.   The crowning of the Rose Queen in 1934. The children at the school performed this ceremony every year in June and entertained the parents with singing and dancing.

115. A Band of Hope treat outside Aston Hall. Colonel MacLean of Aston Hall, standing on the left side of the porch, used to put the grounds of Aston Hall at the disposal of the Sunday schools and the Band of Hope, even erecting swings in the trees for the children to play on.

SHROPSHIRE.

THE ASTON HALL ESTATE,

IN THE PARISH OF SHIFFNAL.

PARTICULARS OF THE VALUABLE

FREEHOLD ESTATE,

CALLED "THE ASTON HALL ESTATE,"

CONSISTING OF A COMMODIOUS AND CONVENIENT

FAMILY MANSION,

Containing Entrance Hall, Dining and Drawing Rooms, Morning Room, 12 Bedrooms, & 4 Dressing Rooms,

WITH EXCELLENT

WALLED AND OTHER GARDENS,

Yards, Double Coach House, Stables for 7 Horses, & excellent Out Offices, with

453 ACRES OF

Meadow, Pasture & Arable Land,

POOLS AND PLANTATIONS,

WITH SUBSTANTIAL RESIDENCE & FARM BUILDINGS,

SITUATED IN THE PARISH OF SHIFFNAL, IN SHROPSHIRE,

ALSO FOUR PEWS IN SHIFFNAL CHURCH,

To be Sold by Auction,

BY MR. WILLIAM HALL,

AT THE LION HOTEL, SHREWSBURY,

On Friday, the 13th day of October, 1865,

At 3 o'Clock in the Afternoon, subject to conditions to be then declared.

The Timber to be taken to at a valuation.

The Estate is Freehold, (except about half an acre portion of No. 50, which is held under a lease expiring in 1882, at a reserved rent of £1 13s. 0d.) and the whole as will be seen by the Plan lies conveniently together, and not intermixed with the Lands of other Proprietors, and will be offered in one Lot.

116.   This sale notice for Aston Hall in 1865, when the MacLean family bought it, has many interesting details. The 453 acres mentioned is probably the whole of the original township lands which were given to Battlefield College in 1410 and sold by the Crown to the Jobber family who emparked it in the 16th century. Note also that the sale included pews in Shifnal church.

117. For a few years in the early 1920s Haughton Hall, formerly the home of the Brooke family (*see* plate 25), was a private girls' school. The picture shows the teachers in the grounds. During the Second World War, Haughton Hall was taken over by Dr. Barnardo's. Since the war it has served as a county council boarding school for children with learning difficulties. This school recently closed and the Hall again now houses a private school.

118. These are the children of the Haughton Hall School in the 1920s enacting a pageant called 'The Seasons'.

119. Maypole dancing and the crowning of the May Queen on the May Field, Haughton Lane, around 1913. Miss F. Currie, then infant headmistress, used to train the children for this ceremony every year until about 1920.

120. One of the surviving bills sent to the committee which arranged a dinner to celebrate Queen Victoria's Golden Jubilee in 1887.

THE ASTON BAKERY,
ASTON STREET, SHIFNAL,
June 21 1887

M Dinner Committee
Bought of C. & H. EDWARDS,
BREAD & BISCUIT BAKERS, CONFECTIONERS, &c.

Groceries, Teas, Coffees, and Provisions.   *All kinds of Pig Feeds.*

	£	s	d
Roasting 7 Rounds of Beef @ 6/ Each		3	6
For Past & Covering Same		2	6
	£	6	0

Settled June 24
1887. C. Edwards

HIGH STREET, SHIFNAL,

June 1887

To Mr Clark

Bought of J. R. WAKELAM,

COOPER, &c.

DEALER IN GLASS, CHINA AND EARTHENWARE.

PICTURES FRAMED & MOUNTED.

1887

June 21 Hire of Dinner Ware for Jubilee			
500 Dinner Plates 6 doz	1	0	0
500 Glasses & Jugs 6 „	1	0	0
60 Saucers 3 „		1	3
4 Plates short		1	0
6 „ Chipped		1	0
17 Glasses short & Broken		6	4
4 Jug Broken		1	0
£	2	11	9

Paid 9th 1887

Wakelam
with thanks

121b. This cup and saucer with views of Shifnal was sold by the firm of Wakelam who supplied the china for the Golden Jubilee dinner. They began dealing in china and glass in the 1880s, though the coopery side of the business was older. The firm continued trading until about the end of the First World War.

122.   The Market Place decorated for Queen Victoria's Diamond Jubilee in 1897.

123.   A crowd in the Market Place outside the station in 1901 at the end of the Boer War. They were welcoming the returning troops.

124. Tom Doyle home on leave during the First World War. He was a dispatch rider and, though wounded in the face by a sniper's bullet, survived the war.

125. The voluntary nurses, V.A.D.s, and the wounded soldiers at Hatton Grange when it was used as a hospital during the First World War.

SHIFNAL PARISH COUNCIL.

Notice is hereby given that a reward of **10/-** will be given to anyone who will give such information as will lead to the conviction of any person or persons who has willfully damaged three of the seats under the Railway Bridge, Market Place, and at Upton.

Notice is hereby further given that the seats placed in various parts of the Town are for the use only of wounded Soldiers.

By Order of the Council,

Benj. Farmer.

May, 1918.

D. Hall, Junr., Printer, Shifnal.

126. This sad and interesting poster proclaims that the seats around the town were only for the use of wounded soldiers. The casualties were known locally as the 'Blue Boys'.

127. A crowd gathered in Bradford Street on Armistice Day, 11 November 1918, to hear the announcement of the end of the First World War.

128. Miss F. Currie, headmistress of the infants, leading the children in a First World War victory parade.

129.   Princess Mary and Viscount Lascelles photographed at Shifnal station after their wedding in 1922. The Girl Guides form the guard of honour.

130. The crowds in Aston Street waiting to cheer Princess Mary and Viscount Lascelles as they travelled from the station to Weston Park for their honeymoon.

131. A group of children in Fullerton's yard off the Broadway near Spencer's smithy in 1920.
Mr. Fullerton pursued the unusual occupation of horse breaker.

132.   Rev. Giles taking the salute for the Warship Week march past during the Second World War. Standing beside the Rev. Giles is George Robey, the famous music hall comedian, self-styled 'prime minister of mirth'. Warship Week was held to encourage saving for the war effort.

133.   The fire brigade taking part in the same parade with their new fire engine. The chief of the fire brigade was Jack Dyke who used to play the cinema piano during the silent films.

134. A meet of the Albrighton Hounds in the Market Place. The hounds last met in the Market Place in 1935.

135. Shifnal cricket team in the 1920s. Cricket has been popular in Shifnal for many years. The club was formed in 1849 and used a field in Haughton Lane. They moved to their present grounds in 1871, and recently a bowling green and tennis courts have been added on the site. The present club house was opened by Sir Len Hutton in 1968.

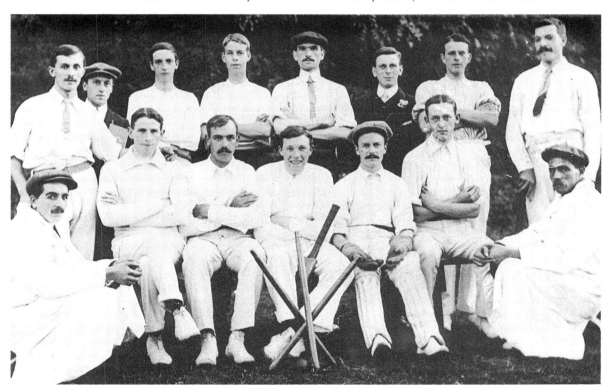

136. St Andrew's Bible Class football team in 1922 with Mr. T.C. Smith, saddler (*see* no. 35), who ran a very successful boys' and men's bible class for many years.

137.   Shifnal Church of England School netball team in 1925 with their teachers, Mr. L. Bingham and Miss Gladys Bruce.

138.   The men's doubles during a three-day tennis tournament held on the cricket field sometime during the 1930s. These tournaments were held annually to raise funds for the cottage hospital.

139. Matron's dance in the 1930s. Every year the matron of the cottage hospital arranged a dance in St Andrew's Hall to raise money for the hospital.

140. This cottage in Haughton Lane was known as the Nurse's Cottage in the 1930s because the district nurse lived there. The cottage belonged to the Brooke family, once of Haughton Hall, and providing it for the nurse was just one example of the family's philanthropy.

141. The Girl Guides in 1929 with their captain, Miss S. Swinburne, and their lieutenant, Miss M. Dakin. By 1929 the number of Guides had risen so they met in a building behind the Baptist chapel in Shrewsbury Road.

142.   The Guides at a camp fire on the Mound in 1929. This Mound, the remains of the moated homestead of the Dunstanvilles, was near the vicarage garden and was a favourite spot for camp fires.

143. The Girl Guides in 1920. Their leaders, seated in the centre of the picture, were Mrs. J.K. Swinburne, the vicar's wife, and Miss White, governess at the vicarage. There had been a slightly earlier group in Shifnal, but it was these ladies who put Guiding on a firm footing. The Guides met in the vicarage garden or in the vicarage schoolroom.

144. The Brownies in 1929 with their Brown Owl, Miss M. Dakin, and their Tawny Owls, Miss C. Newman and Miss D. Barnes. They met in a large room at Idsall House in Park Street, then Dr. Legge's house, now a hotel.

145. The Rover Scouts, Scouts and Cubs in the vicarage garden in 1929. The Cub leader was Mrs. M. Legge, and the scout leaders were Dr. F. Kennedy and the Rev. J.K. Swinburne. Dr. Kennedy was a keen supporter of scouting and established the movement in Shifnal. He converted a cottage behind Marshall's shop in the Market Place for the Scouts to use as a 'den'.

146. The Shifnal bellringers in 1906. Shifnal has eight bells cast in 1770. The famous change-ringer, Steadman, rang his first peal outside London in Shifnal. Samuel Lawrence was a keen bellringer in the Shifnal team at the turn of the 18th and 19th centuries; he kept an illustrated record of the peals he played at different churches around the country.

About this time the following persons did ring 1008 B Major on the Hand bells at the house of Mrs Sarah Nock, Shiffnal. Standing as follows.

Jno Nock ——— 1- 2 in the Parlour
Jno Debney ——— 3- 4 — „ Bruhouse
Samᵉ Lawrence. 5- 6 — „ Up stairs
Thoˢ Aimson 7- 8 — Cellar (Called)

AT SHIFFNAL CHURCH.
23ʳᵈ April 1785.
10,080. B:MAJOR in 6 Hours and 30 Minutes.

Thoˢ Yates	Treble	John Cooper	5ᵗʰ
John Holding	2	Thoˢ Sandford	6ᵗʰ
John Downing	3	Andrew Peake	7ᵗʰ
Richᵈ Amies	4ᵗʰ	Samᵉ Lawrence	Tenor

Called by Andrew Peake.

147. Two pages from Samuel Lawrence's book. Notice that the hand bell players are in different rooms – synchronisation must have been difficult. At 32 stone, Samuel Lawrence was reputed to be the second largest man in England at the time, and he once stuck on the belfry steps of St Alkmund's, Shrewsbury. He was being carried in his special chair to his coach when it collapsed and he was fatally injured.

148. The church choir in 1919. The vicar, seated in the middle, was the Rev. J.K. Swinburne. Mr. A. Roberts, next to the vicar, was organist and choirmaster for many years.

149. Shifnal choir at the station in 1933 on the way to sing at the Crystal Palace.

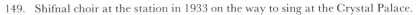

150. Shifnal choir in 1948 with the churchwardens seated at the front. The church choir has been an enduring feature of Shifnal life, and its standard has remained extremely high.

151. A scene from a pageant in the 1930s. The pageant was held in St Andrew's Hall on the Broadway on behalf of the Waifs and Strays Society.

152.   The cast of the same pageant which was performed throughout in mime.

153. This amateur production was the entertainment at a parish social in the late 1940s. These annual socials were important local occasions when the hall at the Institute was crowded for the tea, entertainment and the report on the church finances by the vicar. The food was donated and prepared by volunteers, and the funds raised were given to the church.

154. The dramatic society in J.B. Priestley's *When We Are Married*. This was said to have been the most popular amongst their many popular productions. People from all walks of life enjoyed this society, which sadly no longer exists.

155. The Shifnal choristers' orchestra. This orchestra was trained by the organist and choirmaster. The children are standing outside the church room built in 1923. The land for this hall was another gift of the Brooke family.

156. The band in a later revival (*see* no. 104) wearing their new uniforms. They practised at the *Unicorn Inn* and also at the *Old Bell*. For many years they led the Club Day procession. This is another group which no longer exists, though there has been a recent attempt to revive the band.

157. The golf club at Brimstree Hill. The land was given to Shifnal in the 1850s by the Slaney family of Hatton Grange, and was laid out as pleasure grounds at that time. The golf course which came later was, however, only a 9-hole course, and in the 1960s the club raised the money to buy Deckerhill Hall and lay out a full-size course.

158. A Women's Institute outing in the 1950s. The Women's Institute has been popular in Shifnal since 1922. At that time they met at the Institute and paid 2d. per meeting for a cup of tea and a scone.

159. A chapel outing soon after the Second World War. Trentham Gardens was a favourite destination at that time.

160.   A group of old Shifnal residents. There are memorial tablets in the church which record the unusually long lives of several people, including William Wakely and Mary Yates, who were both said to have lived to over 120 years of age. The combined age of the group in this photograph was over 400 years.